CONTENTS

INTRODUCTION

Definition of Lead Generation

Lead generation refers to the process of identifying and attracting potential customers, known as leads, for a business's products or services. It involves various marketing strategies and tactics designed to capture the interest and contact information of individuals who have shown a potential interest in what a business offers. These leads can then be nurtured and converted into paying customers. In essence, lead generation is about creating opportunities for businesses to connect with their target audience and build relationships that can ultimately drive sales.

Lead generation can be accomplished through various channels, both online and offline. Common methods include content marketing, email marketing, social media marketing, search engine optimization (SEO), events, and advertising. The goal is to capture leads' information, such as their names, email addresses, phone numbers, and other relevant details, which can be used for further communication and sales efforts.

Importance of Lead Generation for Businesses

Lead generation plays a crucial role in the success and growth of businesses. Here are several reasons why it is important:

1. **Increased Sales Opportunities**: By generating leads, businesses create more opportunities to convert potential customers into paying

customers. With a steady stream of qualified leads, sales teams can focus their efforts on engaging with prospects who have already shown interest, increasing the chances of closing deals.

2. **Targeted Marketing**: Lead generation allows businesses to specifically target their ideal customer profile. By understanding their target audience's demographics, preferences, and pain points, businesses can tailor their marketing messages and campaigns to resonate with potential leads, leading to higher conversion rates.

3. **Cost-Effective**: Compared to traditional advertising methods, lead generation can be a cost-effective approach. Instead of broadcasting messages to a broad audience and hoping for a response, businesses can invest their marketing budget in strategies that directly reach individuals who are more likely to be interested in their offerings. This targeted approach reduces wasted resources and maximizes the return on investment.

4. **Relationship Building**: Lead generation is not just about acquiring customers; it's also about building relationships. By providing valuable content and engaging with leads at different stages of the buyer's journey, businesses can establish trust and credibility. This fosters long-term relationships and increases the likelihood of repeat business and referrals.

5. **Data Collection and Analysis**: Lead generation allows businesses to gather valuable data

about their target audience. By tracking and analyzing lead behavior, businesses can gain insights into their customers' needs, preferences, and pain points. This data can then be used to refine marketing strategies, personalize communication, and improve overall business performance.

Overview of Wishpond as a Lead Generation Tool

Wishpond is a comprehensive lead generation tool that helps businesses attract, engage, and convert leads. It offers a wide range of features and functionalities designed to streamline the lead generation process. Here are some key aspects of Wishpond:

1. **Landing Pages**: Wishpond provides a user-friendly drag-and-drop landing page builder that allows businesses to create high-converting landing pages without the need for coding or design skills. These landing pages can be optimized for lead capture, promoting specific offers or events, and driving traffic to the website.

2. **Forms and Pop-ups**: Wishpond enables businesses to create customized forms and pop-ups to capture lead information. These can be embedded on landing pages, websites, or blogs to encourage visitors to provide their contact details in exchange for valuable content, exclusive offers, or subscriptions.

3. **Contests and Promotions**: Wishpond offers tools to run contests, sweepstakes, and promotions, which are effective in attracting leads and

increasing engagement. Businesses can create viral giveaways, social media contests, and referral programs to incentivize lead participation and sharing.

4. **Email Marketing**: Wishpond includes email marketing automation features to nurture leads and drive conversions. Businesses can create personalized email campaigns, segment their leads based on behavior and demographics, and automate follow-ups to keep leads engaged and move them through the sales funnel.

5. **Social Media Marketing**: Wishpond integrates with popular social media platforms, allowing businesses to run targeted ad campaigns, create social media contests, and capture leads directly from social media channels. This helps businesses expand their reach and engage with their target audience where they spend their time.

6. **Analytics and Reporting**: Wishpond provides in-depth analytics and reporting features to track the performance of lead generation campaigns. Businesses can measure conversion rates, analyze lead behavior, and optimize their strategies based on data-driven insights.

Purpose and Benefits of the Guide

The purpose of this guide is to provide businesses with a comprehensive understanding of lead generation and how Wishpond can be utilized as an effective lead generation tool. By exploring the topics discussed above, businesses can gain insights into the definition and importance of lead generation, as well as the specific features and functionalities offered by Wishpond.

The guide aims to empower businesses to leverage lead generation strategies to attract, engage, and convert leads, ultimately driving sales and business growth. By implementing the best practices outlined in the guide and utilizing Wishpond's capabilities, businesses can optimize their lead generation efforts and maximize their return on investment.

The benefits of this guide include:

1. **Knowledge Expansion**: Businesses will gain a deeper understanding of lead generation, its significance, and how it fits into their overall marketing strategy. This knowledge can inform decision-making and resource allocation to achieve better results.

2. **Practical Guidance**: The guide offers practical tips, strategies, and examples to help businesses implement effective lead generation campaigns. It provides step-by-step instructions on using Wishpond's features and showcases real-world use cases to inspire and guide businesses in their lead generation efforts.

3. **Efficiency and Effectiveness**: By utilizing Wishpond as a lead generation tool, businesses can streamline their processes, save time, and achieve better results. The guide highlights the key features and benefits of Wishpond, enabling businesses to make informed decisions about incorporating it into their marketing stack.

4. **Measurable Results**: With the help of Wishpond's analytics and reporting capabilities, businesses

can measure the performance of their lead generation campaigns and track key metrics. This allows for data-driven decision-making, optimization, and continuous improvement of lead generation strategies.

CHAPTER ONE
Understanding Lead Generation

What is Lead Generation?

Lead generation is a crucial aspect of marketing that involves the process of identifying and cultivating potential customers for a business's products or services. It refers to the initiation of consumer interest or inquiry into a particular company's offerings. The primary goal of lead generation is to capture the attention of potential customers and convert them into qualified leads, who can then be further nurtured and guided through the sales funnel.

In the modern business landscape, where competition is fierce and customers have numerous options, effective lead generation strategies are essential to ensure sustainable growth and success. Businesses employ various tactics and channels to generate leads, including digital marketing, content creation, social media engagement, events, and more. The process of lead generation typically involves multiple stages, starting from initial awareness and interest to ultimately converting leads into loyal customers.

Types of Leads

1. Marketing Qualified Leads (MQLs)

Marketing Qualified Leads (MQLs) are potential customers who have shown a certain level of interest in a company's products or services based on their interactions with marketing efforts. MQLs are typically identified through lead scoring, which assigns values to different actions or behaviors exhibited by prospects.

To better understand MQLs, let's consider an example. Suppose a software company offers a free e-book on their website, and visitors can download it by providing their contact information. When a visitor completes this action, they become an MQL. The software company can then engage with these leads through targeted marketing campaigns, nurturing them further until they are ready to be passed to the sales team as Sales Qualified Leads (SQLs).

2. **Sales Qualified Leads (SQLs)**

Sales Qualified Leads (SQLs) are prospects who have been determined to be ready for direct engagement with the sales team based on specific criteria, such as their level of interest, budget, authority, and need (commonly referred to as BANT criteria). SQLs have a higher likelihood of converting into paying customers compared to MQLs.

Once an MQL meets the predetermined criteria set by the marketing and sales teams, they are passed on to the sales team for direct follow-up. The sales team then focuses on nurturing the SQLs further, understanding their pain points, offering personalized solutions, and guiding them through the final stages of the sales process, with the ultimate goal of closing a deal and converting them into customers.

Importance of Lead Generation

Effective lead generation plays a vital role in the growth and success of businesses for several reasons:

1. **Business Growth:** Lead generation is the foundation for business growth, as it identifies potential customers and enables businesses to

focus their marketing and sales efforts on those with the highest likelihood of conversion. By targeting the right audience, businesses can maximize their resources and increase their chances of acquiring new customers.

2. **Sales Efficiency:** Generating quality leads ensures that sales teams spend their time and effort on prospects who are genuinely interested in the products or services being offered. This increases the efficiency of the sales process, allowing sales representatives to focus on building relationships, addressing concerns, and closing deals.

3. **Cost-Effective Marketing:** Lead generation helps optimize marketing budgets by targeting specific segments of the market most likely to convert. Instead of employing blanket marketing strategies, businesses can leverage lead generation techniques to reach their ideal customers, reducing costs and increasing return on investment (ROI).

4. **Customer Insights:** Lead generation provides valuable insights into customer behavior, preferences, and pain points. By analyzing the data collected during the lead generation process, businesses can refine their marketing strategies, tailor their offerings, and improve their overall customer experience.

5. **Sustainable Revenue:** By consistently generating qualified leads, businesses can create a sustainable revenue stream. By nurturing leads and guiding them through the sales funnel, companies can build long-term relationships

with customers, leading to repeat business, referrals, and brand loyalty.

Lead Generation Strategies

To effectively generate leads, businesses employ various strategies and tactics. Here are a few commonly used lead generation strategies:

1. **Content Marketing:** Creating and distributing valuable and relevant content is a powerful lead generation strategy. By producing high-quality blog posts, e-books, videos, and webinars, businesses can attract potential customers who are seeking information and solutions related to their products or services. Content marketing establishes the business as a trusted authority and encourages visitors to provide their contact information in exchange for valuable content.

2. **Email Marketing:** Email marketing remains a highly effective method of lead generation. By building an opt-in email list, businesses can nurture leads by sending targeted and personalized email campaigns. These emails can include relevant content, special offers, product updates, and other valuable information to keep leads engaged and move them closer to making a purchase.

3. **Social Media Marketing:** Social media platforms offer vast opportunities for lead generation. By creating compelling and engaging content, interacting with followers, and utilizing targeted advertising, businesses can attract potential customers and encourage them to provide their

contact information or engage in conversations that can lead to conversions.

4. **Search Engine Optimization (SEO):** Optimizing websites and content for search engines is crucial for lead generation. By implementing SEO best practices, businesses can improve their visibility in search engine results, drive organic traffic to their website, and capture the attention of potential customers actively searching for solutions or information related to their offerings.

5. **Paid Advertising:** Pay-per-click (PPC) advertising allows businesses to display targeted ads on search engines and social media platforms. By carefully selecting keywords, demographics, and interests, businesses can reach their ideal audience and direct them to dedicated landing pages designed to capture leads.

6. **Webinars and Events:** Hosting webinars and participating in industry events are effective ways to generate leads. By offering valuable insights, education, or live demonstrations, businesses can attract an audience interested in their niche. Webinars and events provide opportunities to collect contact information from attendees and engage with them on a more personal level.

7. **Referral Programs:** Encouraging satisfied customers to refer their friends and colleagues can generate high-quality leads. By incentivizing referrals, businesses tap into their existing customer base's network and gain access to potential customers who are more likely to trust

recommendations from someone they know.

It's important to note that lead generation strategies should be tailored to the specific target audience and industry. A combination of these strategies, along with continuous monitoring, analysis, and optimization, can yield successful results.

Lead Generation Funnel

A lead generation funnel is a marketing concept that represents the customer journey from initial contact with a business to becoming a potential customer or lead. It is a systematic approach to capturing and nurturing leads, ultimately leading to conversions and sales. The funnel is divided into three stages: Top of the Funnel (TOFU), Middle of the Funnel (MOFU), and Bottom of the Funnel (BOFU). Each stage plays a vital role in guiding prospects through the sales process. In this article, we will explore each stage of the lead generation funnel and their significance in driving business growth.

Top of the Funnel (TOFU)

The top of the funnel, often referred to as TOFU, is the initial stage where potential customers become aware of your business. At this stage, prospects may be unfamiliar with your brand or have a general interest in the industry. The primary goal of TOFU is to attract a large audience and generate awareness. Here are a few key strategies for the top of the funnel:

1. Content Marketing: Creating valuable content is essential for attracting and engaging prospects. This includes blog posts, videos, infographics, and social media content. By offering informative and relevant content, you can capture the attention of your target audience and establish yourself as an industry authority.

2. Search Engine Optimization (SEO): Optimizing your website for search engines helps improve your organic visibility and drives traffic to your site. Conducting keyword research, optimizing meta tags, and building quality backlinks are all crucial components of effective SEO.

3. Social Media Marketing: Leveraging social media platforms allows you to reach a wider audience and engage with potential customers. By sharing valuable content, running targeted ads, and actively participating in relevant communities, you can attract prospects and encourage them to learn more about your business.

4. Lead Magnets: Offering valuable resources such as e-books, whitepapers, or free guides in exchange for contact information can help capture leads at the top of the funnel. These lead magnets provide value to prospects while allowing you to nurture the relationship and move them further down the funnel.

Middle of the Funnel (MOFU)

The middle of the funnel, known as MOFU, is where prospects move from being aware of your brand to displaying interest and considering your products or services. At this stage, you have captured their attention, and now it's time to nurture the relationship and provide more targeted information. Here are some strategies for the middle of the funnel:

1. Email Marketing: Email campaigns are an effective way to nurture leads and build trust. Sending personalized and relevant content to prospects helps keep your brand top of mind and encourages them to move forward in the buyer's journey.

2. Lead Nurturing: Develop a lead nurturing strategy that includes tailored content for different buyer personas. This can involve providing case studies, product comparisons, or testimonials that address specific pain points and showcase the value of your offerings.

3. Webinars and Events: Hosting webinars or attending industry events provides opportunities to engage with prospects directly. These platforms allow you to showcase your expertise, address common questions, and build relationships with potential customers.

4. Retargeting: Utilize retargeting techniques to reach prospects who have shown interest in your brand but have not converted. By displaying targeted ads on various platforms, you can remind them of your offerings and encourage them to take the next step.

Bottom of the Funnel (BOFU)

The bottom of the funnel, also referred to as BOFU, is the stage where leads are primed for conversion. At this point, prospects have shown a high level of interest and are ready to make a purchasing decision. Here are some strategies to optimize the bottom of the funnel:

1. Personalized Offers: Tailor your offers and promotions based on the prospect's behavior and preferences. Use data and analytics to provide personalized recommendations and discounts that incentivize conversions.

2. Product Demonstrations: Offering product demos or free trials allows prospects to experience your offerings firsthand. This hands-on approach helps alleviate any concerns or hesitations they may have, increasing the likelihood of conversion.

3. Customer Testimonials: Showcase positive reviews and testimonials from satisfied customers. Social proof plays a crucial role in instilling trust and confidence in prospects, giving them the final nudge to convert.

4. Streamlined Conversion Process: Ensure that the conversion process is seamless and user-friendly. Simplify forms, provide multiple payment options, and eliminate any friction that may deter prospects from completing the purchase.

By implementing effective strategies at each stage of the lead generation funnel, businesses can optimize their marketing efforts and increase conversions. Remember, the key is to continuously analyze and refine your approach based on data and feedback from your target audience.

Key Metrics for Measuring Lead Generation Success

Lead generation is a critical aspect of any business's marketing strategy. It involves attracting and capturing potential customers' interest in order to convert them into paying customers. To assess the effectiveness of lead generation efforts, several key metrics can be utilized. This article will explore three essential metrics for measuring lead generation success: conversion rates, cost per lead (CPL), and return on investment (ROI).

Conversion Rates

Conversion rates provide valuable insights into how successful a lead generation campaign is in terms of turning leads into customers. The conversion rate is calculated by dividing the number of conversions (i.e., the number of leads that have completed a desired action, such as making a purchase or filling out a contact form) by the total number of leads generated, and then multiplying the result by 100 to get a percentage.

Factors Affecting Conversion Rates:

1. **Quality of Leads**: The quality of leads generated plays a significant role in determining conversion rates. Higher-quality leads, who are genuinely interested in the product or service, are more likely to convert into customers.

2. **Call-to-Action (CTA) Effectiveness**: The design and placement of CTAs on landing pages or advertisements can impact conversion rates. Well-crafted and compelling CTAs have the potential to drive higher conversion rates.

3. **User Experience (UX)**: The ease of navigation, clarity of information, and overall user experience on websites or landing pages can influence conversion rates. A seamless and user-friendly experience can increase the likelihood of conversions.

4. **A/B Testing**: Conducting A/B tests on different variations of landing pages, CTAs, or ad copies can help identify the most effective elements that drive higher conversion rates.

By monitoring and analyzing conversion rates over time, businesses can assess the success of their lead generation campaigns and make informed decisions to optimize their strategies.

Cost per Lead (CPL)

Cost per lead (CPL) is a metric that measures the average

cost incurred to generate a single lead. It is calculated by dividing the total cost of lead generation efforts by the number of leads generated during a specific period.

Factors Affecting CPL:

1. **Advertising Channels**: The choice of advertising channels, such as social media advertising, search engine marketing, or content marketing, can significantly impact CPL. Each channel has its own cost structure and effectiveness in generating leads.

2. **Target Audience**: The specific target audience and their characteristics can influence CPL. Niche markets or highly competitive industries may require more targeted and cost-intensive lead generation strategies.

3. **Campaign Optimization**: Continuous monitoring and optimization of lead generation campaigns can help reduce CPL. By identifying underperforming elements and adjusting the strategy accordingly, businesses can improve efficiency and reduce costs.

4. **Lead Quality**: The quality of leads generated is closely related to CPL. Low-quality leads that are unlikely to convert can inflate the overall cost per lead. Focusing on attracting high-quality leads can help optimize CPL.

By analyzing CPL, businesses can assess the cost-effectiveness of their lead generation efforts and allocate resources efficiently to achieve maximum ROI.

Return on Investment (ROI)

Return on investment (ROI) is a crucial metric for evaluating the overall success and profitability of lead generation campaigns. It measures the return generated from the money invested in lead generation activities.

Factors Affecting ROI:

1. **Revenue per Customer**: The average revenue generated per customer is a vital factor in calculating ROI. Understanding the lifetime value of customers and their purchasing patterns helps determine the revenue impact of lead generation efforts.

2. **Conversion Rates**: As mentioned earlier, conversion rates have a direct impact on ROI. Higher conversion rates result in more customers, leading to increased revenue and improved ROI.

3. **CPL and Cost Optimization**: Minimizing CPL and optimizing lead generation costs contributes to improved ROI. Efficient allocation of resources and budget management are essential for achieving a positive return on investment.

4. **Marketing and Sales Alignment**: The alignment between marketing and sales teams is crucial for maximizing ROI. Collaboration and effective communication ensure that leads generated by marketing efforts are effectively converted into paying customers by the sales team.

Tracking ROI enables businesses to determine the profitability of their lead generation initiatives and make data-driven decisions to optimize their marketing strategies.

CHAPTER TWO

Wishpond Overview

Introduction to Wishpond as a Lead Generation Platform

Wishpond is a powerful lead generation platform that provides businesses with a comprehensive suite of marketing tools to attract, engage, and convert leads. It offers a range of features and capabilities designed to streamline marketing campaigns, increase customer acquisition, and drive revenue growth. In this article, we will explore the key aspects of Wishpond and how it can benefit businesses in their lead generation efforts.

Features and Capabilities of Wishpond

Landing Page Builder

One of the standout features of Wishpond is its robust landing page builder. With a user-friendly drag-and-drop interface, businesses can easily create professional and visually appealing landing pages without any coding or design skills. Wishpond offers a wide variety of customizable templates that can be tailored to match a brand's unique style and messaging.

Key points about the landing page builder:

- Intuitive drag-and-drop interface for easy page creation
- Customizable templates for quick and professional designs
- Mobile-responsive pages for seamless user experience

- A/B testing functionality to optimize conversion rates
- Integration with CRM and email marketing platforms for efficient lead management

Forms and Pop-ups

Wishpond provides a range of form options to capture visitor information and convert them into leads. From simple contact forms to more advanced multi-step forms, businesses can choose the form type that best suits their needs. Additionally, Wishpond offers customizable pop-ups that can be strategically placed on websites to capture visitors' attention and drive conversions.

Key points about forms and pop-ups:

- Various form types, including contact forms, lead capture forms, and survey forms
- Conditional logic to show or hide form fields based on user responses
- Pop-up customization options for different website sections
- Exit-intent pop-ups to reduce bounce rates and increase conversions
- Integration with email marketing tools for seamless lead nurturing

Email Marketing Automation

Wishpond's email marketing automation features enable businesses to create targeted and personalized email campaigns to engage and nurture leads. The platform offers a visual email editor that allows users to design visually appealing emails without any coding knowledge. Businesses can set up automated workflows triggered by user actions, such as form submissions or email opens, to deliver timely and relevant content to their audience.

Key points about email marketing automation:

- Visual email editor for creating professional and personalized emails
- Automated workflows based on user behavior and triggers
- Segmentation and tagging capabilities for targeted campaigns
- A/B testing for email subject lines, content, and CTAs
- Performance tracking and reporting to measure campaign success

Social Media Contests and Promotions

Wishpond enables businesses to run engaging social media contests and promotions to increase brand visibility, drive social engagement, and capture leads. The platform provides tools to create and manage contests on popular social media platforms like Facebook, Instagram, and Twitter. Businesses can design contests with customizable entry forms, voting mechanisms, and sharing incentives to encourage participants to spread the word.

Key points about social media contests and promotions:

- Contest creation and management across multiple social media platforms
- Customizable entry forms to collect participant information
- Voting mechanisms and sharing incentives to increase reach
- Integration with social media advertising platforms for boosted campaigns

- Automated winner selection and prize fulfillment

Marketing Analytics and Tracking

Wishpond offers comprehensive marketing analytics and tracking capabilities to measure the success of campaigns and optimize marketing strategies. Businesses can track key metrics such as website visits, conversions, email open rates, and social media engagement. The platform provides detailed reports and analytics dashboards that offer valuable insights into campaign performance, enabling businesses to make data-driven decisions.

Benefits of using Wishpond for lead generation

Wishpond is a powerful lead generation tool that offers a wide range of benefits to businesses. In this article, we will explore three key advantages of using Wishpond for lead generation: a streamlined lead capture process, automation and personalization capabilities, and integration with other marketing tools.

Streamlined lead capture process

One of the primary benefits of using Wishpond for lead generation is its streamlined lead capture process. Wishpond provides businesses with a user-friendly platform that allows them to create and customize attractive landing pages, pop-ups, and forms to capture leads effectively.

1. **Ease of use:** Wishpond's drag-and-drop editor makes it incredibly easy for businesses to create professional-looking landing pages without requiring any coding or design skills. This empowers businesses of all sizes to quickly set up lead capture campaigns and start generating leads.

2. **Customization options:** Wishpond offers a wide range of customization options, enabling businesses to align their lead capture forms and landing pages with their brand identity. From colors and fonts to images and background settings, businesses have the flexibility to create a cohesive and visually appealing experience for their potential leads.

3. **Responsive design:** Wishpond ensures that all lead capture assets are responsive and optimized for different devices and screen sizes. This means that businesses can reach and engage potential leads across desktops, tablets, and mobile devices, providing a seamless experience for users regardless of their preferred device.

By simplifying the lead capture process, Wishpond helps businesses increase conversions and capture more high-quality leads.

Automation and personalization

Wishpond goes beyond basic lead capture functionalities by offering robust automation and personalization features. These features allow businesses to automate their lead nurturing efforts and deliver targeted, personalized experiences to their leads.

1. **Email marketing automation:** Wishpond provides businesses with powerful email automation tools that enable them to create personalized email campaigns based on user behavior, demographics, and engagement. Businesses can set up automated email sequences to nurture leads, deliver targeted content, and

drive conversions.

2. **Dynamic content:** Wishpond allows businesses to create dynamic landing pages and forms that adapt and change based on the visitor's profile, preferences, or previous interactions. This level of personalization enhances the user experience and increases the chances of capturing qualified leads.

3. **Lead scoring and segmentation:** Wishpond's lead scoring and segmentation capabilities help businesses prioritize and categorize leads based on their level of engagement and interest. By segmenting leads into different groups, businesses can tailor their marketing messages and campaigns, ensuring that the right message reaches the right audience at the right time.

By leveraging automation and personalization, businesses can save time, deliver relevant content, and build stronger relationships with their leads, ultimately driving higher conversion rates.

Integration with other marketing tools

Another significant benefit of using Wishpond for lead generation is its seamless integration with other marketing tools. Wishpond integrates with popular marketing platforms and CRMs, allowing businesses to centralize their lead generation efforts and streamline their marketing workflows.

1. **CRM integration:** Wishpond integrates with leading CRM platforms such as Salesforce, HubSpot, and Mailchimp. This integration enables businesses to sync their leads directly to their CRM, ensuring a smooth handover from

marketing to sales and providing a holistic view of the customer journey.

2. **Email marketing integration:** Wishpond integrates with email marketing platforms like Mailchimp, Constant Contact, and AWeber, allowing businesses to sync their leads and seamlessly incorporate them into their email marketing campaigns. This integration ensures that businesses can effectively nurture leads and drive conversions through targeted email communication.

3. **Analytics and tracking integration:** Wishpond integrates with popular analytics and tracking tools, such as Google Analytics and Facebook Pixel. This integration provides businesses with valuable insights into their lead generation campaigns, allowing them to measure the effectiveness of their strategies, optimize their conversion funnels, and make data-driven decisions.

By integrating with other marketing tools, Wishpond empowers businesses to leverage their existing infrastructure, enhance their lead generation capabilities, and achieve a more comprehensive and efficient marketing ecosystem.

CHAPTER THREE
Creating a Lead Generation Strategy with Wishpond

Setting Goals for Lead Generation

Setting clear and measurable goals is crucial for effective lead generation. Without defined objectives, it becomes challenging to track progress and make informed decisions. When establishing goals for lead generation, it is important to consider the specific needs and objectives of your business. Here are some key points to consider when setting goals for lead generation:

1. **Define your objectives**: Start by clearly defining what you want to achieve through lead generation. Are you looking to increase brand awareness, generate a certain number of leads, or drive conversions? Identifying your primary objective will help you align your efforts and focus your resources.

2. **Quantify your goals**: Once you have defined your objective, quantify it with specific targets. For example, if your goal is to generate leads, set a target number of leads you want to generate within a given timeframe. This will provide a clear benchmark to measure your progress against.

3. **Make goals realistic and achievable**: While it's important to set ambitious goals, it's equally crucial to ensure they are realistic and achievable.

Consider your available resources, market conditions, and historical data to set goals that are challenging yet attainable.

4. **Set a timeline**: Establish a timeline for achieving your lead generation goals. Determine whether your goals are short-term or long-term, and break them down into actionable milestones. Having a timeline helps create a sense of urgency and keeps your team focused and motivated.

5. **Track and measure progress**: Implement a robust tracking system to monitor your progress towards your lead generation goals. Use key performance indicators (KPIs) such as conversion rates, website traffic, and lead quality to measure the effectiveness of your lead generation efforts. Regularly review and analyze the data to make informed adjustments to your strategies.

By setting clear and measurable goals for lead generation, you provide a direction for your marketing efforts, motivate your team, and enable effective tracking and optimization of your lead generation campaigns.

Identifying Target Audience and Buyer Personas

To maximize the effectiveness of your lead generation efforts, it is essential to identify your target audience and create detailed buyer personas. Understanding your audience allows you to tailor your marketing messages, offers, and strategies to resonate with their specific needs and preferences. Here's how you can identify your target audience and develop buyer personas:

1. **Conduct market research**: Start by conducting thorough market research to gather insights

about your industry, competitors, and target market. Use tools like surveys, interviews, and social media listening to gather valuable data about your potential customers.

2. **Analyze existing customer data**: Analyze your existing customer data to identify patterns, trends, and characteristics of your ideal customers. Look for common demographics, interests, pain points, and purchasing behaviors.

3. **Segment your audience**: Once you have gathered sufficient data, segment your audience based on relevant criteria such as demographics, psychographics, and behaviors. This segmentation helps you create more personalized and targeted marketing campaigns.

4. **Create buyer personas**: Develop detailed buyer personas based on your audience segments. A buyer persona is a fictional representation of your ideal customer, incorporating information such as age, gender, job title, goals, challenges, and preferred communication channels. Use this persona to guide your marketing strategies and content creation.

5. **Validate and refine**: Continuously validate and refine your buyer personas as you gather more data and insights. Stay updated with market trends, conduct surveys, and engage with your audience to ensure your personas accurately represent your target customers.

By identifying your target audience and developing buyer personas, you can tailor your lead generation strategies to effectively reach and engage the right people, increasing the chances of generating high-quality leads.

Creating Compelling Offers and Lead Magnets

Compelling offers and lead magnets play a crucial role in attracting and capturing leads. These are incentives or valuable resources that you offer to potential customers in exchange for their contact information. To create compelling offers and lead magnets, consider the following tips:

1. **Understand your audience's needs**: Identify the pain points, challenges, and aspirations of your target audience. What are they looking for? What problems are they trying to solve? Use this understanding to create offers that address their specific needs and provide value.

2. **Offer valuable content**: Develop high-quality content that educates, informs, or entertains your audience. This could include e-books, whitepapers, guides, templates, checklists, or exclusive access to resources. Ensure that your content is actionable, relevant, and solves a problem for your audience.

3. **Create compelling headlines**: Craft attention-grabbing headlines that clearly communicate the benefits of your offer. Use persuasive language and focus on the outcome or transformation your audience can expect by accessing your offer.

4. **Design visually appealing assets**: Invest in professional design and ensure that your offers and lead magnets are visually appealing. Well-designed assets enhance perceived value and

increase the likelihood of conversion.

5. **Optimize landing pages**: Build dedicated landing pages for your offers and lead magnets. Keep the design clean, use persuasive copywriting, and include clear calls-to-action (CTAs) to encourage visitors to take the desired action.

6. **Implement lead capture forms**: Include lead capture forms on your landing pages to collect contact information from your leads. Keep the form fields concise and relevant, asking for the minimum required information to minimize friction and maximize conversions.

Remember to regularly evaluate the performance of your offers and lead magnets, make data-driven optimizations, and test different variations to improve your lead generation efforts.

Designing High-Converting Landing Pages and Forms

Landing pages and forms are critical elements in lead generation campaigns. Well-designed landing pages and forms can significantly impact conversion rates and the overall success of your lead generation efforts. Here are some best practices for designing high-converting landing pages and forms:

1. **Keep it simple and focused**: Design your landing pages with simplicity in mind. Avoid clutter and distractions that can divert visitors' attention. Keep the page focused on a single offer or message to avoid confusion.

2. **Craft compelling headlines and copy**: Use persuasive and benefit-driven headlines to capture visitors' attention. Clearly communicate

the value proposition of your offer and highlight the key benefits. Use concise and compelling copy to engage your audience and guide them towards the desired action.

3. **Use eye-catching visuals**: Incorporate visually appealing images, videos, or graphics to enhance the visual appeal of your landing page. Visuals can help convey your message more effectively and create a positive impression.

4. **Optimize for mobile devices**: With the increasing use of mobile devices, it is essential to ensure that your landing pages are mobile-friendly. Optimize the design and layout for smaller screens, and ensure fast loading times for a seamless mobile experience.

5. **Include clear and prominent CTAs**: Place clear and prominent calls-to-action (CTAs) on your landing pages. Use contrasting colors, compelling copy, and strategic placement to draw attention to your CTA buttons. Make sure the CTAs are concise, action-oriented, and easily distinguishable.

6. **Minimize form fields**: Keep your lead capture forms concise and straightforward. Only ask for the essential information you need to follow up with leads effectively. Long forms can discourage conversions, so aim to minimize the number of fields to increase form completion rates.

7. **Leverage trust indicators**: Incorporate trust indicators such as customer testimonials, reviews, security badges, or trust seals to build trust and credibility. These elements reassure

visitors that their information is secure and that your offer is reliable.

8. **Optimize page loading speed**: Slow-loading pages can lead to high bounce rates and lost conversions. Optimize your landing pages by compressing images, minimizing scripts, and utilizing caching techniques to ensure fast loading times.

9. **A/B test and optimize**: Implement A/B testing to experiment with different variations of your landing pages and forms. Test elements such as headlines, visuals, CTAs, form fields, and overall layout to identify what resonates best with your audience. Continuously monitor the results and make data-driven optimizations to improve conversion rates.

10. **Provide a seamless user experience**: Ensure a seamless user experience by designing intuitive navigation, clear information hierarchy, and easy-to-understand form instructions. Visitors should be able to navigate your landing pages effortlessly and complete the form submission process without confusion.

By implementing these best practices, you can create high-converting landing pages and forms that effectively capture leads and drive successful lead generation campaigns.

Implementing Email Marketing Campaigns

Email marketing remains a powerful tool for lead generation and nurturing. Implementing effective email marketing campaigns allows you to engage with your leads, build relationships, and guide them through the buyer's journey. Here are some key steps to consider when implementing email marketing campaigns:

1. **Segment your email list**: Divide your email list into segments based on criteria such as demographics, interests, previous interactions, or purchase history. Segmenting allows you to send more personalized and relevant messages, increasing engagement and conversions.

2. **Craft compelling subject lines**: Your subject line plays a crucial role in determining whether your emails get opened or ignored. Create attention-grabbing subject lines that are concise, clear, and compelling. Experiment with personalization, urgency, or curiosity to increase open rates.

3. **Create valuable and relevant content**: Develop content that provides value to your subscribers. Share informative blog posts, industry insights, how-to guides, case studies, or exclusive offers. Tailor your content to align with the interests and pain points of your audience segments.

4. **Use a conversational tone**: Write your emails in a conversational tone to establish a connection with your subscribers. Avoid overly promotional language and focus on building trust and rapport. Use personalization tokens to address subscribers by their name and make the emails feel more personalized.

5. **Include clear CTAs**: Each email should have a clear and compelling call-to-action (CTA). Whether it's directing subscribers to download an

e-book, register for a webinar, or make a purchase, the CTA should be prominently displayed and encourage action.

6. **Optimize for mobile**: Ensure that your emails are optimized for mobile devices. The majority of people read emails on their smartphones, so it's important to have responsive designs that adapt to different screen sizes. Test your emails across various devices and email clients to ensure a seamless experience.

7. **Automate your campaigns**: Implement marketing automation to streamline your email marketing campaigns. Set up automated workflows triggered by specific actions or events, such as welcome emails, abandoned cart reminders, or post-purchase follow-ups. Automation saves time, increases efficiency, and allows for timely and targeted communication.

8. **Monitor and analyze performance**: Regularly monitor the performance of your email campaigns. Track metrics such as open rates, click-through rates, conversion rates, and unsubscribe rates. Analyze the data to identify trends, optimize your campaigns, and improve engagement and conversion rates.

Remember to adhere to email marketing best practices, including obtaining proper consent, providing clear unsubscribe options, and following relevant regulations like GDPR or CAN-SPAM Act.

Optimizing Lead Nurturing and Follow-Up Processes

Lead nurturing is the process of building relationships

with potential customers and guiding them through the sales funnel. Optimizing lead nurturing and follow-up processes is essential to keep leads engaged and move them closer to making a purchase. Here are some strategies to optimize your lead nurturing efforts:

1. **Develop a lead scoring system**: Implement a lead scoring system to prioritize and identify high-quality leads. Assign values to various lead attributes and behaviors to gauge their level of interest and readiness to purchase. This scoring system helps you focus your resources on the most promising leads.

2. **Segment and personalize your communications**: Segment your leads based on their attributes, interests, and engagement level. Tailor your communications to each segment, delivering content that resonates with their specific needs. Personalization enhances the relevance and effectiveness of your nurturing efforts.

3. **Create targeted and valuable content**: Develop a content strategy that aligns with the different stages of the buyer's journey. Provide educational and informative content that addresses the pain points and challenges of your leads. Use a mix of formats such as blog posts, videos, webinars, or case studies to cater to different preferences.

4. **Use marketing automation**: Leverage marketing automation tools to streamline and personalize your lead nurturing workflows. Set up automated drip campaigns that deliver timely and relevant content based on triggers and actions taken by your leads. Automation saves time, ensures

consistency, and allows for timely follow-ups.

5. **Integrate marketing and sales efforts**: Foster alignment between your marketing and sales teams to ensure a seamless transition of leads from marketing to sales. Establish clear handoff criteria and communication channels to facilitate smooth lead transfers. Collaboration and feedback between the teams help optimize the lead nurturing process.

6. **Monitor engagement and adjust**: Continuously monitor the engagement levels of your leads. Track metrics such as email opens, click-through rates, website visits, and content downloads. Identify leads that require additional nurturing or are ready for a sales conversation. Adjust your nurturing strategies based on the feedback and engagement data.

7. **Personalize the sales follow-up**: When leads reach a stage where they are ready for direct sales follow-up, ensure that the interaction is personalized and tailored to their specific needs. Use the insights gathered during the lead nurturing process to have informed and relevant conversations that drive conversion.

Remember that lead nurturing is an ongoing process that requires consistent effort and refinement. By optimizing your lead nurturing and follow-up processes, you can build stronger relationships with your leads and increase the chances of converting them into loyal customers.

Leveraging Social Media for Lead Generation

Social media platforms provide a vast opportunity for lead

generation and brand awareness. Leveraging social media effectively allows you to reach a wider audience, engage with potential customers, and drive traffic to your website or landing pages. Here are some strategies for leveraging social media for lead generation:

1. **Choose the right platforms**: Identify the social media platforms that align with your target audience's preferences and behaviors. Focus your efforts on platforms where your potential customers are most active. Popular platforms for lead generation include Facebook, Instagram, LinkedIn, Twitter, and YouTube.

2. **Optimize your profiles**: Optimize your social media profiles to reflect your brand identity and provide relevant information. Use consistent branding elements, compelling descriptions, and links to your website or landing pages. Ensure that your profiles are visually appealing and represent your brand in a professional manner.

3. **Create valuable content**: Develop content that is valuable, informative, and shareable. Craft posts, articles, images, videos, or infographics that resonate with your target audience. Share content that educates, entertains, or solves a problem for your followers. Consistently provide value to establish trust and credibility.

4. **Engage with your audience**: Actively engage with your social media audience by responding to comments, messages, and mentions. Encourage discussions, ask questions, and participate in relevant conversations. Show genuine interest in your audience's opinions and feedback. Engaging

with your audience fosters a sense of community and strengthens relationships.

5. **Utilize social media advertising**: Consider running targeted social media advertising campaigns to reach a wider audience and generate leads. Platforms like Facebook and LinkedIn offer robust advertising tools that allow you to define specific targeting criteria and create compelling ad creatives. Experiment with different ad formats, audiences, and messaging to optimize your campaigns.

6. **Incorporate lead generation tactics**: Use social media to drive traffic to your landing pages or lead capture forms. Share links to gated content, webinars, or exclusive offers that require visitors to provide their contact information. Direct users to dedicated landing pages optimized for lead generation.

7. **Run contests and giveaways**: Conduct social media contests or giveaways to encourage user participation and generate leads. Ask users to enter the contest by providing their email addresses or other contact information. This tactic not only generates leads but also creates buzz and increases brand visibility.

8. **Collaborate with influencers**: Identify relevant influencers or industry experts who have a significant following on social media. Collaborate with them through sponsored posts, guest content, or joint campaigns to tap into their audience and expand your reach. Influencer collaborations can help generate leads and build

credibility.

9. **Monitor and analyze metrics**: Regularly monitor and analyze the performance of your social media efforts. Track metrics such as engagement rate, reach, click-through rates, and conversions. Use social media analytics tools to gain insights into the effectiveness of your lead generation strategies and make data-driven optimizations.

10. **Encourage social sharing**: Implement social sharing buttons on your website, landing pages, and content assets. Make it easy for visitors to share your content with their networks, expanding your reach and potentially attracting new leads. Encourage social sharing by creating valuable and shareable content that resonates with your audience.

By effectively leveraging social media platforms, you can reach a broader audience, engage with potential leads, and drive traffic to your lead generation assets.

Tracking and Measuring Lead Generation Results

Tracking and measuring the results of your lead generation efforts is essential for evaluating the effectiveness of your strategies and making data-driven decisions. Here are key steps to effectively track and measure lead generation results:

1. **Establish key performance indicators (KPIs)**: Identify the metrics that align with your lead generation goals. Common KPIs include the number of leads generated, conversion rates, cost per lead, lead quality, and return on investment (ROI). Establishing KPIs helps you set benchmarks

and track progress.

2. **Implement analytics tools**: Utilize analytics tools such as Google Analytics, CRM systems, or marketing automation platforms to gather data and insights. Set up tracking codes, tags, and goals to capture relevant information about website traffic, conversions, and lead interactions.

3. **Track the customer journey**: Follow the customer journey from the initial touchpoint to conversion. Implement attribution models that track how leads interact with your marketing channels and campaigns throughout their journey. This allows you to identify the most effective touchpoints and optimize your marketing efforts.

4. **Monitor conversion funnels**: Set up conversion funnels to track the steps a lead takes before converting. Analyze where leads drop off in the funnel and identify potential bottlenecks or areas for improvement. Optimize the user experience and streamline the conversion process to increase conversion rates.

5. **Implement UTM parameters**: Use UTM parameters in your campaign URLs to track the performance of specific marketing campaigns, channels, or mediums. This allows you to attribute leads and conversions to specific sources and measure the effectiveness of different marketing initiatives.

6. **Conduct A/B testing**: Experiment with different variations of your marketing campaigns, landing pages, forms, or email subject lines through A/

B testing. Split your audience and compare the performance of different elements to identify what resonates best with your target audience. Use the insights gained to optimize your lead generation strategies.

7. **Generate regular reports**: Generate regular reports that provide an overview of your lead generation performance. Include key metrics, trends, and insights that inform decision-making. Share these reports with stakeholders to ensure transparency and alignment with business objectives.

8. **Analyze lead quality**: In addition to quantity, assess the quality of the leads generated. Monitor lead engagement, conversion rates, and sales outcomes to determine the effectiveness of your lead generation strategies. Adjust your targeting, messaging, and nurturing efforts to attract and convert higher-quality leads.

9. **Integrate data sources**: Integrate data from different sources, such as CRM systems, marketing automation platforms, and social media analytics, to get a holistic view of your lead generation efforts. Connecting the data allows for more accurate analysis and a comprehensive understanding of your performance.

10. **Continuously optimize**: Regularly review and analyze the data to identify trends, patterns, and areas for improvement. Use the insights gained to optimize your lead generation strategies, refine targeting, adjust messaging, and allocate resources effectively.

By tracking and measuring lead generation results, you can gain valuable insights into the performance of your campaigns, identify areas for improvement, and make data-driven decisions to enhance your lead generation efforts.

Remember that lead generation is an iterative process, and continuous tracking, analysis, and optimization are key to achieving long-term success.

CHAPTER FOUR

Advanced Techniques for
Maximizing Lead Generation

A/B Testing and Optimization Strategies

A/B testing and optimization strategies are essential components of any successful marketing campaign. By conducting A/B tests, marketers can compare two versions of a webpage, email, or advertisement to determine which one performs better in terms of engagement, conversion rates, or other desired metrics. This allows marketers to make data-driven decisions and optimize their marketing efforts. Here are some key points to consider when implementing A/B testing and optimization strategies:

1. **Objective Setting**: Before conducting an A/B test, it is crucial to define clear objectives. Whether it is increasing click-through rates, improving conversion rates, or enhancing user engagement, setting specific goals helps focus the test and measure its success accurately.

2. **Variable Selection**: Identify the variables that you want to test. These variables can include elements such as headlines, images, call-to-action buttons, color schemes, or even layout. Ensure that the variables you select have a significant impact on user behavior and can be easily modified.

3. **Sample Size Determination**: Determine an appropriate sample size for your A/B test to ensure statistical significance. A larger sample

size minimizes the margin of error and provides more reliable results. Various online calculators and statistical tools can assist in determining the required sample size based on the desired level of confidence and expected effect size.

4. **Randomization**: Randomly assign users to the different variations of your A/B test to avoid any bias. Randomization helps ensure that the results are not skewed by factors like user preferences or demographics.

5. **Data Collection and Analysis**: Collect data on user interactions, conversions, or other relevant metrics throughout the duration of the A/B test. Analyze the data using statistical methods to determine which variation performs better. Common statistical techniques used for A/B testing include t-tests, chi-square tests, and regression analysis.

6. **Iterative Testing and Optimization**: A/B testing should be an ongoing process. Once you have identified a winning variation, it is important to continue testing and optimizing further. Small incremental changes can lead to significant improvements over time.

7. **Multivariate Testing**: In addition to A/B testing, consider implementing multivariate testing when you want to test multiple variables simultaneously. Multivariate testing allows you to analyze the combined impact of different variables on user behavior and identify the most effective combination.

8. **User Experience Considerations**: While A/B testing focuses on improving specific metrics, it is essential to keep the overall user experience in mind. Changes that negatively impact user experience, even if they improve a specific metric, may lead to long-term negative effects on customer satisfaction and retention.

By implementing effective A/B testing and optimization strategies, marketers can continuously refine their campaigns, increase conversions, and drive better results.

Personalization and Segmentation Tactics

Personalization and segmentation tactics enable marketers to tailor their messages and offers to specific audience segments, enhancing relevance and engagement. By understanding their customers' preferences, behaviors, and demographics, marketers can deliver targeted content that resonates with each segment. Here are some key tactics to consider when implementing personalization and segmentation strategies:

1. **Data Collection and Analysis**: Collect and analyze relevant customer data to gain insights into their preferences, behaviors, and demographics. This data can be collected through various channels, including website analytics, customer surveys, social media monitoring, and purchase history. Use this data to segment your audience effectively.

2. **Segmentation Criteria**: Determine the segmentation criteria based on your business goals and customer characteristics. Segments can be defined by factors such as demographics, psychographics, purchase history, browsing

behavior, or engagement levels. Consider using a combination of criteria to create more refined and targeted segments.

3. **Dynamic Content**: Implement dynamic content delivery based on user segmentation. This involves creating personalized content variations that align with the preferences and characteristics of each segment. Dynamic content can be applied to website landing pages, email campaigns, product recommendations, and personalized offers.

4. **Email Personalization**: Use personalized email marketing strategies to enhance engagement and conversion rates. Personalize email subject lines, greetings, and content based on the recipient's name, past purchases, browsing history, or other relevant data. Leverage automation tools to efficiently manage and scale personalized email campaigns.

5. **Website Personalization**: Tailor the website experience based on user segments. Implement dynamic content, personalized recommendations, and targeted offers to create a more personalized and engaging website journey. Use cookies and user tracking to recognize returning visitors and present them with relevant content.

6. **Behavioral Trigger Campaigns**: Set up automated campaigns triggered by specific user behaviors or events. For example, if a user abandons their shopping cart, you can send a personalized email offering a discount to encourage them

to complete the purchase. Behavioral trigger campaigns help nurture leads and drive conversions.

7. **Social Media Targeting**: Leverage social media platforms' targeting capabilities to reach specific audience segments. Utilize features such as custom audiences, lookalike audiences, and interest-based targeting to deliver personalized messages to the right people at the right time.

8. **Testing and Optimization**: Continuously test and optimize personalization and segmentation tactics to improve results. A/B testing can be applied to personalized content, subject lines, calls-to-action, and other elements to identify the most effective strategies for each segment.

By implementing personalized and segmented marketing tactics, marketers can deliver more relevant and engaging experiences, leading to increased customer satisfaction, loyalty, and conversions.

Lead Scoring and Qualification Methods

Lead scoring and qualification methods help marketers identify and prioritize leads based on their likelihood to convert into customers. These methods involve assigning scores to leads based on their demographic data, behaviors, and engagement levels. By focusing their efforts on high-quality leads, marketers can optimize their resources and improve conversion rates. Here are some key methods for lead scoring and qualification:

1. **Define Lead Scoring Criteria**: Start by defining the criteria that indicate a qualified lead for your business. This can include factors such as job

title, industry, company size, geographic location, website interactions, email engagement, and content downloads. Assign different weights or scores to each criterion based on its importance.

2. **Behavioral Tracking**: Use website analytics and marketing automation tools to track user behavior and engagement. Monitor actions such as page visits, time spent on site, content downloads, email opens, click-through rates, and form submissions. These behaviors can provide insights into a lead's level of interest and engagement.

3. **Lead Source Analysis**: Analyze the sources from which leads are generated to identify high-performing channels. Different lead sources may have varying conversion rates and quality levels. By understanding the most effective lead sources, marketers can allocate their resources and budget accordingly.

4. **Lead Scoring Models**: Develop lead scoring models to assign scores or rankings to individual leads based on their attributes and behaviors. Models can be simple or complex, depending on the business's requirements and available data. Consider using machine learning algorithms to automate and optimize lead scoring processes.

5. **Lead Qualification Questions**: Incorporate lead qualification questions into your lead capture forms or qualification processes. These questions can help gather additional data to assess a lead's fit and intent. For example, asking about budget, timeline, or specific pain points can

provide valuable insights into a lead's readiness to purchase.

6. **Marketing and Sales Alignment**: Establish a close collaboration between marketing and sales teams to define shared lead scoring and qualification criteria. Regularly review and update these criteria based on feedback and insights from the sales team. This alignment ensures that marketing efforts are focused on generating leads that have a higher chance of converting into customers.

7. **Lead Nurturing**: Implement lead nurturing campaigns to engage and educate leads throughout their buyer's journey. Use marketing automation tools to deliver personalized content and targeted messaging based on a lead's score and stage in the sales funnel. Lead nurturing helps build relationships, address objections, and move leads closer to making a purchase.

8. **Continuous Evaluation and Optimization**: Continuously evaluate the effectiveness of your lead scoring and qualification methods. Analyze the conversion rates, sales outcomes, and customer feedback associated with different lead scores and qualification criteria. Use this information to refine your models and optimize your lead management processes.

By implementing effective lead scoring and qualification methods, marketers can focus their efforts on leads with the highest potential for conversion, resulting in improved efficiency, increased sales, and better return on investment.

Retargeting and Remarketing Strategies

Retargeting and remarketing strategies are powerful techniques for re-engaging potential customers who have shown interest in your products or services but have not yet made a purchase. These strategies involve delivering targeted advertisements to users who have visited your website, interacted with your brand, or abandoned their shopping carts. Here are some key strategies to consider when implementing retargeting and remarketing campaigns:

1. **Pixel Implementation**: Install retargeting pixels or tags on your website to track user interactions and behavior. These pixels enable you to identify and segment users who have shown interest in specific products or sections of your site. This information is used to deliver personalized ads to these users across various platforms.

2. **Segmentation and Audience Creation**: Segment your website visitors and users based on their behavior and engagement levels. Create custom audiences for different segments, such as visitors who abandoned their carts, engaged with specific content, or showed interest in particular products. This segmentation allows you to tailor your retargeting campaigns to each audience segment.

3. **Dynamic Product Ads**: Implement dynamic product ads that showcase the specific products or services that users have viewed or added to their carts. These ads are highly personalized and create a sense of familiarity, reminding users of their previous interest and encouraging them to

complete their purchase.

4. **Abandoned Cart Recovery**: Target users who have abandoned their shopping carts with personalized ads and reminders. Offer incentives such as discounts, free shipping, or limited-time promotions to entice them to return and complete their purchase. Automated email sequences can also be used to remind users of their abandoned carts and provide additional incentives.

5. **Cross-Sell and Upsell Campaigns**: Use retargeting and remarketing campaigns to promote complementary or upgraded products to users who have made a previous purchase. By analyzing their purchase history and browsing behavior, you can identify relevant upsell or cross-sell opportunities and create targeted ads to promote these offerings.

6. **Frequency Capping**: Set frequency caps to control the number of times a user sees your retargeting ads. Displaying ads too frequently can lead to ad fatigue and annoyance. By limiting the frequency, you ensure that your ads stay relevant and impactful without overwhelming the user.

7. **Audience Exclusions**: Exclude users who have already converted or shown disinterest to avoid wasting ad spend on irrelevant audiences. Regularly review and update your exclusion lists to optimize your retargeting campaigns and focus on high-potential prospects.

8. **Performance Monitoring and Optimization**: Continuously monitor the performance of your

retargeting and remarketing campaigns. Analyze key metrics such as click-through rates, conversion rates, and return on ad spend (ROAS). Use this data to refine your targeting strategies, ad creatives, and bidding strategies for better results.

Retargeting and remarketing strategies help keep your brand top of mind, re-engage potential customers, and drive them back to your website for conversion. By delivering personalized and relevant ads, you can significantly increase your chances of converting those who have previously shown interest in your products or services.

Integration with CRM Systems

Integration with Customer Relationship Management (CRM) systems is crucial for aligning marketing and sales efforts, streamlining data management, and enhancing customer insights. By integrating your marketing tools and CRM system, you can achieve a seamless flow of data, improve lead management, and gain a holistic view of your customers. Here are some key benefits and considerations when integrating marketing systems with CRM:

1. **Data Synchronization**: Ensure that contact, lead, and customer data seamlessly sync between your marketing tools and CRM system. This synchronization enables accurate lead tracking, lead nurturing, and customer segmentation based on real-time data. It also eliminates manual data entry and reduces the risk of data discrepancies.

2. **Lead Handoff and Sales Alignment**: Integrate lead scoring, qualification, and tracking systems

between marketing and sales teams. This integration allows for efficient lead handoff, ensuring that marketing-generated leads are promptly and appropriately passed on to the sales team. The integration also enables better coordination, visibility, and collaboration between marketing and sales efforts.

3. **Closed-Loop Reporting**: Leverage CRM integration to track and attribute marketing activities to revenue and customer acquisition. Closed-loop reporting provides insights into the effectiveness of marketing campaigns, lead sources, and customer journeys. It enables you to measure return on investment (ROI) and optimize marketing strategies based on revenue outcomes.

4. **Enhanced Customer Insights**: By integrating marketing systems with CRM, you can access comprehensive customer profiles that include data from multiple touchpoints. This integrated view allows for a deeper understanding of customer behavior, preferences, and interactions with your brand. It enables personalized marketing, targeted messaging, and better customer segmentation.

5. **Automated Workflows**: Use CRM integration to automate workflows and streamline marketing processes. For example, automatically update lead statuses, trigger personalized email sequences based on CRM events, or assign tasks to sales representatives based on lead activities. Automation reduces manual effort, ensures consistency, and improves efficiency.

6. **Lead Scoring and Nurturing**: Integrate CRM data into your lead scoring and nurturing processes. By combining CRM data with marketing data, such as email engagement or website interactions, you can create more accurate lead scoring models and deliver targeted content to nurture leads based on their stage in the customer journey.

7. **Campaign Attribution**: Attribute marketing campaigns and activities to specific leads, opportunities, or closed deals within the CRM system. This attribution allows you to analyze the impact of different marketing channels, campaigns, and touchpoints on revenue generation. It helps you understand which marketing efforts are most effective in driving conversions.

8. **Data Privacy and Security**: Ensure that the integration between your marketing systems and CRM complies with data privacy regulations and follows best practices for data security. Protecting customer data and maintaining privacy is of utmost importance to build trust with your audience and avoid potential legal or reputational issues.

By integrating your marketing systems with CRM, you can optimize lead management, align marketing and sales efforts, gain valuable customer insights, and improve the overall efficiency and effectiveness of your marketing campaigns.

Leveraging Marketing Automation for Lead Nurturing

Marketing automation plays a vital role in lead nurturing

by delivering personalized and timely content to leads at various stages of the customer journey. It allows marketers to automate repetitive tasks, nurture leads with relevant information, and move them closer to making a purchase. Here are some key strategies for leveraging marketing automation and marketing automation for lead nurturing:

1. **Lead Scoring and Segmentation**: Utilize marketing automation tools to implement lead scoring models and segment your leads based on their behavior, demographics, and engagement levels. This segmentation allows you to deliver targeted content and personalized experiences to different groups of leads, ensuring relevance and effectiveness.

2. **Automated Email Campaigns**: Set up automated email campaigns that are triggered based on specific lead actions or predefined timelines. For example, send a welcome email series to new leads, nurture leads who have downloaded a content offer with a series of educational emails, or send re-engagement emails to leads who have become inactive. These automated campaigns help deliver the right message to the right leads at the right time.

3. **Dynamic Content Personalization**: Leverage marketing automation platforms to dynamically personalize the content of your emails and landing pages based on lead attributes and behaviors. By tailoring the content to match each lead's specific interests and needs, you can significantly improve engagement and conversion rates.

4. **Lead Nurturing Workflows**: Create nurturing workflows that guide leads through the customer journey, providing them with relevant content and offers at each stage. These workflows can include a combination of emails, social media interactions, personalized landing pages, and triggered events. The goal is to educate and build trust with leads, positioning your brand as a valuable resource.

5. **Behavior-Based Triggers**: Implement behavior-based triggers within your marketing automation platform to deliver personalized messages based on specific lead actions. For instance, if a lead visits a product page multiple times, you can automatically send them a targeted offer or provide additional information to help them make a purchase decision. These triggers allow for real-time responsiveness and personalized engagement.

6. **Lead Nurturing Analytics**: Monitor and analyze the performance of your lead nurturing campaigns using the analytics capabilities of your marketing automation platform. Track metrics such as email open rates, click-through rates, conversion rates, and overall campaign effectiveness. Use these insights to refine your nurturing strategies and optimize your campaigns for better results.

7. **Multi-Channel Lead Nurturing**: Extend your lead nurturing efforts beyond email marketing by utilizing other channels such as social media, SMS, or push notifications. By incorporating

multiple touchpoints, you can engage leads through their preferred channels and create a cohesive and personalized experience across various platforms.

8. **Sales and Marketing Alignment**: Foster collaboration and alignment between your sales and marketing teams to ensure seamless lead handoff and a consistent nurturing process. Regularly communicate and share insights on lead behavior, feedback, and sales outcomes to refine your lead nurturing strategies and optimize the handoff between marketing and sales.

By leveraging marketing automation for lead nurturing, you can deliver personalized, timely, and relevant content to your leads, nurture them throughout their buyer's journey, and increase the likelihood of conversion. It allows you to build stronger relationships with your leads, enhance their customer experience, and ultimately drive revenue growth.

Collaborating with Influencers and Affiliates

Collaborating with influencers and affiliates can be an effective strategy to expand your reach, build credibility, and drive conversions. Influencers are individuals who have a significant following and influence over a particular target audience, while affiliates are individuals or organizations that promote your products or services in exchange for a commission. Here are some key considerations when collaborating with influencers and affiliates:

1. **Identify Relevant Influencers and Affiliates**: Research and identify influencers and affiliates

whose target audience aligns with your target market. Look for individuals or organizations that have a genuine connection with your industry, niche, or product category. Consider their reach, engagement levels, and the authenticity of their audience.

2. **Establish Clear Goals and Expectations**: Clearly define your goals for the collaboration, whether it's to increase brand awareness, drive website traffic, generate leads, or boost sales. Communicate your expectations to the influencers or affiliates, including the desired deliverables, key messages, and any specific guidelines or requirements.

3. **Compensation and Incentives**: Determine the compensation or incentives for the influencers or affiliates. This can be in the form of monetary payment, free products or services, exclusive discounts or promotions, or a commission-based structure. Ensure that the compensation aligns with the value they provide and the desired outcomes of the collaboration.

4. **Authenticity and Relevance**: Seek influencers or affiliates whose values and content align with your brand. Authenticity and relevance are crucial for maintaining credibility and resonating with their audience. Choose collaborators who genuinely believe in your products or services and can provide authentic recommendations or endorsements.

5. **Content Collaboration**: Collaborate with influencers and affiliates to create engaging and

relevant content that highlights your brand, products, or services. This can include sponsored blog posts, social media mentions, product reviews, or guest appearances on podcasts or webinars. Co-creating content ensures that it aligns with their audience's interests while promoting your brand effectively.

6. **Trackable Links and Discount Codes**: Provide influencers and affiliates with trackable links or unique discount codes to monitor the performance and effectiveness of their promotional efforts. These tracking mechanisms allow you to measure the traffic, conversions, and sales generated through their influence or promotion.

7. **Engagement and Relationship Building**: Actively engage with influencers and affiliates throughout the collaboration process. Regularly communicate with them, provide necessary support or resources, and acknowledge their contributions. Building strong relationships with collaborators can lead to long-term partnerships and mutually beneficial outcomes.

8. **Performance Evaluation**: Continuously evaluate the performance and impact of your collaborations. Monitor key metrics such as website traffic, engagement rates, conversion rates, and sales attributed to the influencers or affiliates. Analyze the return on investment (ROI) to assess the effectiveness of different collaborations and optimize future partnerships.

By collaborating with influencers and affiliates, you can tap into their existing audience, leverage their credibility, and amplify your brand's reach. It allows you to connect with new prospects, build trust, and drive conversions through trusted recommendations and endorsements.

Generating Leads through Content Marketing

Content marketing is a strategic approach to attract, engage, and convert your target audience by creating and distributing valuable, relevant, and consistent content. It plays a crucial role in generating leads and nurturing them through the buyer's journey. Here are some key strategies for generating leads through content marketing:

1. **Targeted Content Creation**: Create content that specifically caters to your target audience's needs, challenges, and interests. Conduct thorough research to understand their pain points, frequently asked questions, and the type of content they prefer. Develop a content strategy that includes blog posts, ebooks, whitepapers, videos, infographics, or webinars that address their specific needs.

2. **Optimize for Search Engines**: Implement search engine optimization (SEO) techniques to ensure your content ranks well in search engine results. Use relevant keywords, meta tags, and descriptive headlines to make your content more discoverable. High-quality, optimized content can attract organic traffic and generate leads.

3. **Lead Magnets and Gated Content**: Offer valuable resources or lead magnets, such as ebooks, guides, templates, or exclusive industry reports, in exchange for contact information. Use landing

pages and opt-in forms to capture leads' details and gradually nurture them with relevant content.

4. **Guest Blogging and Thought Leadership**: Contribute guest posts to authoritative websites or publications within your industry. This allows you to tap into their audience and establish yourself as a thought leader in your niche. Include links back to your website or landing pages to drive traffic and capture leads.

5. **Email Marketing**: Utilize email marketing campaigns to promote your content and capture leads. Build an email list by offering newsletter subscriptions, content updates, or exclusive access to additional resources. Send regular emails to nurture leads, provide valuable insights, and drive them back to your website.

6. **Social Media Promotion**: Leverage social media platforms to promote your content and engage with your target audience. Share snippets of your content, create visually appealing graphics or videos, and encourage social sharing. Engage in conversations, respond to comments, and actively participate in relevant communities to expand your reach and attract leads.

7. **Webinars and Online Events**: Host webinars or online events on topics of interest to your target audience. Require attendees to register with their contact information, allowing you to capture leads. Deliver valuable insights, provide interactive experiences, and nurture attendees through the sales funnel with follow-up emails

and additional content.

8. **Content Distribution Channels**: Explore various content distribution channels to expand your reach and attract leads. This can include syndicating your content on industry-specific websites, submitting guest posts to relevant publications, participating in podcasts or video interviews, or partnering with influencers to amplify your content's reach.

9. **Data-driven Optimization**: Continuously analyze the performance of your content marketing efforts and optimize based on data insights. Track key metrics such as website traffic, time on page, click-through rates, conversion rates, and lead generation. Use this data to identify high-performing content, understand audience preferences, and refine your content strategy.

10. **CTA Optimization**: Ensure that your content includes clear and compelling calls-to-action (CTAs) to drive lead generation. Use enticing offers, such as free trials, consultations, or exclusive discounts, to encourage visitors to take the next step. Place CTAs strategically within your content and make them prominent to capture leads effectively.

11. **Marketing Automation**: Integrate marketing automation tools to streamline lead nurturing processes. Set up automated email sequences that deliver relevant content based on lead behavior and engagement. Use marketing automation platforms to segment leads, personalize messaging, and track lead interactions to deliver a

personalized experience.

12. **Interactive Content**: Incorporate interactive content formats, such as quizzes, assessments, interactive infographics, or calculators, into your content marketing strategy. Interactive content not only captures leads but also provides an engaging and interactive experience that can increase conversion rates.

By implementing a comprehensive content marketing strategy, you can attract, engage, and convert leads. Valuable and relevant content positions your brand as an industry authority, builds trust with your audience, and drives meaningful interactions that ultimately result in lead generation and customer acquisition.

Remember to regularly assess and refine your content marketing efforts based on data insights and evolving audience needs to ensure continuous lead generation success.

CONCLUSION

Recap of Key Points Covered in the Guide

In this guide, we have explored various strategies and techniques for effective lead generation using Wishpond. Let's recap the key points covered to ensure a comprehensive understanding of the topic.

1. **Understanding Lead Generation:** We began by defining lead generation and its significance in the business world. Lead generation involves attracting potential customers and converting them into leads, which can eventually lead to sales. Wishpond provides a range of tools and features to facilitate this process.

2. **Creating Engaging Landing Pages:** We discussed the importance of well-designed landing pages that capture visitors' attention and encourage them to take action. Wishpond offers a user-friendly interface to build customizable landing pages that align with your brand and effectively communicate your value proposition.

3. **Optimizing Lead Capture Forms:** We emphasized the need for well-optimized lead capture forms to collect valuable customer information. Wishpond allows you to create and customize forms with ease, making it simple to gather the data you need to nurture and convert leads.

4. **Implementing Effective Call-to-Actions (CTAs):** CTAs play a crucial role in guiding visitors

towards desired actions. We explored various strategies for creating compelling CTAs, such as using action-oriented language, incorporating urgency, and placing them strategically throughout your website. Wishpond provides a range of CTA templates and tools to enhance their effectiveness.

5. **Utilizing Email Marketing:** We highlighted the power of email marketing as a tool for lead nurturing and conversion. Wishpond's email marketing features enable you to segment your audience, personalize your messages, and automate your campaigns, ensuring that your leads receive relevant and timely content.

6. **Leveraging Social Media:** We discussed the importance of incorporating social media into your lead generation efforts. Wishpond allows you to easily create and manage social media contests, promotions, and advertisements, helping you expand your reach and attract new leads.

7. **Tracking and Analyzing Results:** We emphasized the significance of tracking and analyzing the performance of your lead generation campaigns. Wishpond offers robust analytics and reporting features, enabling you to measure the effectiveness of your strategies, identify areas for improvement, and make data-driven decisions.

Final Thoughts on Using Wishpond for Lead Generation

Wishpond provides a comprehensive set of tools and features to streamline your lead generation efforts. By leveraging its capabilities, you can enhance your marketing strategies and drive meaningful results. Here are some final thoughts to consider when using Wishpond for lead generation:

1. **Ease of Use:** Wishpond offers a user-friendly platform that makes it accessible for both beginners and experienced marketers. The intuitive interface and drag-and-drop functionality enable you to create landing pages, forms, and campaigns without requiring extensive technical knowledge.

2. **Customization and Branding:** Wishpond allows you to customize your lead generation assets to align with your brand identity. You can personalize colors, fonts, and imagery to create a consistent brand experience for your audience, fostering trust and recognition.

3. **Integration Capabilities:** Wishpond integrates with various third-party tools, such as CRM systems and email marketing platforms, enabling seamless data transfer and workflow automation. This integration enhances your lead management processes and ensures efficient follow-up with your prospects.

4. **Lead Nurturing:** Wishpond's email marketing and automation features empower you to nurture your leads effectively. By delivering personalized and targeted content to your prospects at the right time, you can build relationships, establish credibility, and guide them through the sales funnel.

5. **Measurable Results:** Wishpond's analytics and reporting functionalities provide valuable insights into the performance of your lead generation campaigns. You can track metrics like conversion rates, engagement levels, and ROI, allowing you to optimize your strategies and achieve better results over time.

In conclusion, Wishpond offers a robust suite of lead generation tools that can significantly enhance your marketing efforts. By implementing the strategies outlined in this guide and leveraging Wishpond's features, you can attract, engage, and convert high-quality leads for your business.

Encouragement to Implement the Strategies Outlined in the Guide

Now that you have gained a comprehensive understanding of lead generation strategies using Wishpond, it is time to take action. Implementing these strategies can have a significant impact on the growth and success of your business. Here is some encouragement to inspire you to implement the strategies outlined in the guide:

1. **Unlock Your Business Potential:** By implementing these lead generation strategies, you have the opportunity to unlock the full potential of your business. Wishpond provides you with the tools and resources to attract and convert leads effectively, allowing you to expand your customer base and drive revenue growth.

2. **Stay Ahead of the Competition:** In today's competitive business landscape, staying ahead of the competition is essential. By leveraging

Wishpond's features and implementing the strategies outlined in this guide, you can differentiate your business and establish a strong presence in your industry.

3. **Build Strong Relationships:** Effective lead generation goes beyond acquiring leads; it involves building strong relationships with your prospects. Wishpond enables you to nurture leads through personalized communication, providing value to your audience and building trust along the way.

4. **Measure, Optimize, and Succeed:** Wishpond's analytics and reporting capabilities allow you to measure the performance of your lead generation campaigns. By analyzing the data and optimizing your strategies based on the insights gained, you can continually improve your results and achieve long-term success.

5. **Take the First Step:** The journey to successful lead generation begins with taking the first step. Don't wait for the perfect moment—start implementing these strategies today. Wishpond's user-friendly platform and comprehensive support resources will guide you along the way.

Remember, effective lead generation is an ongoing process that requires continuous optimization and adaptation. Stay committed to implementing the strategies outlined in this guide, and you will see the positive impact on your business over time.

So, what are you waiting for? Take action, leverage Wishpond, and unlock the full potential of your lead generation efforts.

www.ingramcontent.com/pod-product-compliance
Lightning Source LLC
Chambersburg PA
CBHW060839260726
48661CB00002B/509